THE SECURE FUTURE ADVISOR

Escape the Fatal Tax Traps, Create a Sustainable Income, and Seek to Enjoy an Inflation-Resistant Retirement

THE SECURE FUTURE ADVISOR

*Escape Fatal Tax Traps, Create a
Sustainable Income, and Seek to
Enjoy an Inflation-Resistant Retirement*

MARK A. MORRIS

ethos
collective

THE SECURE FUTURE ADVISOR © 2025 by Mark A. Morris.
All rights reserved.

Printed in the United States of America

Published by Igniting Souls
PO Box 43, Powell, OH 43065
IgnitingSouls.com

This book contains material protected under international and federal copyright laws and treaties. Any unauthorized reprint or use of this material is prohibited. No part of this book may be reproduced or transmitted in any form or by any means, electronic or mechanical, including photocopying, recording, or by any information storage and retrieval system, without express written permission from the author.

LCCN: 2024918908
Paperback ISBN: 978-1-63680-359-3
Hardcover ISBN: 978-1-63680-360-9
e-book ISBN: 978-1-63680-361-6

Available in paperback, hardcover, e-book, and audiobook.

All Scripture quotations, unless otherwise indicated, are taken from the (NASB®) New American Standard Bible®, Copyright © 1960, 1971, 1977, 1995, 2020 by The Lockman Foundation. Used by permission. All rights reserved. lockman.org

All Scripture quotations indicated with NIV are taken from the Holy Bible, New International Version®, NIV®. Copyright © 1973, 1978, 1984, 2011 by Biblica, Inc.™ Used by permission of Zondervan. All rights reserved worldwide. www.zondervan.com The "NIV" and "New International Version" are trademarks registered in the United States Patent and Trademark Office by Biblica, Inc.™

Some scripture taken from the New King James Version® (NKJV). Copyright © 1982 by Thomas Nelson. Used by permission. All rights reserved.

Any Internet addresses (websites, blogs, etc.) and telephone numbers printed in this book are offered as a resource. They are not intended in any way to be or imply an endorsement by Igniting Souls, nor does Igniting Souls vouch for the content of these sites and numbers for the life of this book.

Some names and identifying details may have been changed to protect the privacy of individuals.

Mark A. Morris is the Founder and CEO of Secure Future Advisors LLC and Secure Future Tax Advisors LLC, two separate firms covering subjects from tax planning, investment, retirement income and long-term health care planning.
Mark A. Morris is a Registered Representative of Valmark Securities, Inc., a broker-dealer, Member FINRA, SPIC; and an Investment Advisor Representative with Valmark Advisers, Inc., an SEC registered investment advisor. Secure Future Advisors LLC and Secure Future Tax Planning Advisors LLC are not affiliated with Valmark Securities, Inc. and Valmark Advisors, Inc.

This book is dedicated to my wonderful wife, Kelly and the joy of being a Dad to my nine children. Our clients demand from us a partnership with them in building a more secure future, which this book addresses the necessary planning process and mindset.

CONTENTS

Making the Climb
9

PART ONE
FATALITIES

Chapter One
The Perils of Mountain Climbing
13

PART TWO
FOUNDATION

Chapter Two
Overcoming the Challenges of the Descent
23

Chapter Three
Be On the Lookout for False Gurus
35

Chapter Four
The Secret to Putting the Map Back Together
43

Chapter Five
It's Time to Have a Candid Conversation™
53

Epilogue
63

Endnotes
65

Acknowledgments
69

About the Author
71

MAKING THE CLIMB

They had only descended about one thousand feet when Lola's shrill voice cut the quiet of the snowy summit. Their guide, Anthony, turned just in time to see sixty-five-year-old Mr. Windaker careening down the last five feet to the plateau below.

"Louis, are you alright?" Anthony yelled as he attached a carabiner and rope to his harness. "The wind is blowing this way. I don't think he can hear me," the guide told his partner. What happened?"

"I didn't see him until Mrs. Windaker screamed, so I'm not sure," Finn answered.

"You will have to be my anchor. This incline is pretty steep. I don't think we can get back up here without sliding again unless we have ropes."

"Loooouis! Loooouis!" Mrs. Lola Windaker yelled through her tears.

"Come on, team," Finn told the rest of the climbers. "Split up. Three on each rope. Vincent, you take an anchor point on Louis' rope. Let's get these guys some weight up here so they can climb up this embankment."

With Finn and two other climbers keeping him from moving too quickly down the steep slope, Anthony and his rescue pack began the steep descent down the long snowbank.

Living the Dream

The Windakers had dreamed of climbing Mount Rainier for decades. They started talking about it when they were in college. Louis had a mountaineers' climbing guide on his nightstand, and both walked half a mile every day to stay in shape. So, the year they retired, their children surprised them with airfare, hotels, and access to one of the most qualified guides in Washington state.

Vincent and Vivian Seiger met the Windakers during their first day on Mount Rainier. A movie based on real life had put Mount Rainier in their sights right around their tenth anniversary. The couple had been hiking since their honeymoon and cycled every day, so adding a bit of mountain climbing prep seemed smart.

Since they lived in Vermont, their first climb had been the relatively easy hike offered by Mount Pisgah. For the next ten years, they took on two or three of the easier peaks in the Adirondacks and Alleghenies every year.

During the next five years, Vincent and Vivian upped their game. Even their children—now in their late teens—enjoyed camping at the top of Mount Marcy and Mount Washington. They enlisted guides when they started climbing over 4,000 feet, but they found the knowledge of these men and women worth more than they could have imagined. The descent from those higher altitudes was trickier, and they would have missed hidden eagles' nests and waterfalls just off the trail without the assistance of those escorts.

By the time the last of their kids graduated from high school, the couple was ready for the more challenging climbs. They had to head west to start climbing over 6,000 feet. Camelback and Mount Olympus fed their hunger to hit the higher peaks. When they summited Mount Hood, they felt like Rainier was finally within reach.

PART ONE
FATALITIES

CHAPTER ONE

THE PERILS OF MOUNTAIN CLIMBING

*The mind of man plans his way,
but the Lord directs his steps.*
—Proverbs 16:9

Mountain climbing gives us a good picture of a person's financial life. Our accumulation phase—those years between college and retirement—looks like the ascent. The descent represents the distribution decades—our retirement years. And while most of us have a bit of control over the number of years we can put on the accumulation side of the mountain, the distribution side is as unpredictable as the descent. Without an adequate guide, it can be as dangerous.

Dangerous Crevices

By the time Louis slid down the snowy embankment, it had been five days since the group had gathered at the base of the mountain, so every single person was fighting fatigue—especially the Windakers.

The trip started with two days of training before their ascent. The guides had explained the need for extra care when they reached the glaciers. At an elevation of about

4,000 feet, they would begin to hike across ice that sits atop rivers in Mount Rainier Park. The crevices in the icy surface change daily depending on the temperature and the movement of the water beneath the glaciers. The first two days of the climb would include about six hours of hiking, then making camp on top of one of those ice rivers. "You will need to stay alert and pay close attention to Finn and me as we climb the glaciers. As you can imagine, with the moving crevices and the icy conditions, accidents happen quickly when we don't stay alert."

Anthony hadn't been completely surprised when he'd seen Louis sliding down the mountain. He had predicted the descent would be tough for Louis and Lola. "A few of these climbers might have been a better match for the Disappointment Cleaver route," Anthony had told his partner. Regardless, two couples and two pairs of siblings had opted for the Emmons Ridge adventure—and an adventure it was.

Though they were in good shape for their age, the Windakers obviously didn't realize the strength needed for inclines like those on the Emmons Glacier Trail, and they certainly weren't prepared for the shifting nature of the ice. The six-hour climb each day had taken seven because Louis and Lola required a slower pace than most groups.

During the second night, the team got only a few hours of interrupted sleep. It was about midnight when they heard the warning.

"Come on, everyone up," Finn yelled. "No time to waste. I don't like the noise this glacier is making."

"Can't it wait a few hours? You said we had to get up at four." Louis had to yell to be heard over the howling wind.

Anthony answered. "This spot where your tent sits won't be here in four hours, Louis. Let's get moving, everyone. You have about twenty minutes before this crevice you can see forming is wider than your sleeping bag."

Vincent and Vivian had heard about the ice rivers shifting and changing at a moment's notice. After they got their tent down and repositioned, they helped Louis and Lola secure theirs. The high wind and chill made it challenging, but not any more difficult than falling back to sleep with the moans of the glacier as it moved beneath them.

Like Louis and Lola on Mount Rainier, too many enter retirement with false assumptions regarding Social Security and taxes after they retire. These preconceived notions and vague ideas about Medicare and long-term elderly care are as difficult to maneuver as the crevices in the glaciers on the Emmons Trail. And unfortunately, the bit of knowledge many base their assumptions on is as precarious as assuming you know everything you need to know about mountain climbing from reading the mountaineers' guide every night before you fall asleep.

We constantly look for ways to save on taxes going up the mountain, using as many loopholes as possible to legally keep the amount we pay the IRS as low as possible. Not surprisingly, the IRS is a patient investor, and they'll do whatever they can to separate you from your money. They may have service in their name, but this agency is not in service to retirees. All the tax breaks going up the mountain lull you into a feeling of safety. Few are ready for the countless regulations that reserve all the deadly tax traps for the downward trek.

Eighty years ago, corporations attracted employees by offering booming benefit packages. Many boasted lifetime pension and healthcare. Unfortunately, the last thirty years have shown us most of these big companies either can't or don't want to keep those promises. The simplicity of retiring with a company pension and Social Security no longer exists. Only about twenty percent of working Americans now have a pension plan through their employer, and many of these are public employees.[1]

I'm sure the fact people are living longer partially motivated these businesses to provide large payouts or move to 401(k)s. However, that same fact means retirees who receive a lump sum to compensate them for a lost pension will probably never make enough interest to equal the anticipated pension payments. Now, instead of a guaranteed income, retirees have to make sure their savings will last as long as they do.

Inexperienced Guides

Anthony felt a wave of relief when he saw the moving figure on the ledge below. "Can you get up, Louis?"

"I'm not sure. My arm hurts. But I'm pretty sure I didn't damage anything as badly as my ego."

"Well, let's put the oxygen mask on for just a couple minutes, then I'll take a look at your arm. You may have lost your balance because your brain isn't used to this altitude. Even experienced climbers get tricked by the lack of O2 up here."

Finn and Anthony had encouraged everyone to take advantage of a little extra oxygen while they admired the breathtaking views at the top, but only four of the six who made it to the top had opted to heed the advice. Louis and Lola thought they'd be fine.

After a few minutes of oxygen, Anthony helped Louis take his coat off so he could check the climber's arm. Anthony could see from the swelling that Louis would at least have some bruising from smacking against rocks on the way down. The forearm would need an x-ray when they got back to civilization. The guide wrapped it in a temporary splint to protect it until then.

After awkwardly returning Louis' arm to his coat, Anthony gave him a sling. "Do you think you can make it back to the top? I'll hook the rope to your harness, and you can hold it with your good hand."

"I don't think I have much choice. Do I?"

"Short of bringing in search and rescue, walking up is your only option."

Anthony secured the rope and called to the team waiting at the top, "I think we're ready, Finn. Does everyone have a good footing? You're going to have to pull Louis a bit."

Lola took the third spot on Louis' rope, then Finn called out, "We're set, Anthony. Bring him up."

The two climbers slid several times in the slushy snow, and Louis fell on his face once. Anthony stayed right beside the man, encouraging him and updating the anchor crew at the top with their progress. He and Finn had been through this scenario more than once, so even though their guests were on high alert, the guides felt comfortable with their status.

With a different set of guides, Louis' fall may have turned out much worse. Similarly, it's vital to find the right guide for our financial journey. Not all advisors have the experience and expertise your financial situation needs. The person who helped you in the accumulation phase may not have a specialization in retirement. Many investment managers don't have a wide knowledge of taxes. They focus on what they know best—long-term investing.

The greatest portion of these folks want what's best for you; however, many don't specialize in legal strategies or solutions to reduce your taxes. And even if they have an inkling of what your tax situation will look like after retirement, they don't make money on saving you taxes. Their income depends upon how much of your money they're managing at the moment. Frankly, it is impossible to optimize your retirement lifestyle without tax and investment planning.

The Map in the Blender Approach

Imagine the look on those teams' faces if Anthony or Finn had taken the map and ripped it to shreds before they started their ascent. The arrogant gesture may have sent most of their crew running. Even the most experienced guide keeps a map in their pack for emergencies. Avalanches cause trails to close, and enlarged crevices require a change in navigation.

Still, many plans to conquer financial mountains resemble maps after they've been put in a blender. They have so many different pieces in their financial puzzle they aren't sure which one represents north anymore.

Your grandfather probably worked for the same company for forty years. Today, that's a rarity. People spend four, five, maybe eight years in a position and then move on. And while there's nothing wrong with finding a better job and scaling up, these same individuals often end up with multiple 401(k)s, pensions, and insurance policies they know little about. I call it the "piecemeal approach" to planning.

As you start the mountain descent, a pension may begin, then Social Security. If you're married, both you and your spouse probably have Social Security. Some of your 401(k)s are pre-tax money, and some are post-tax. A few of your investments are with an advising firm, and a few you handle on your own. Each one depends on your situation when it started. And when you begin to gather all the pieces from the blender, you soon realize you aren't sure you have the entire map.

Even the best guide will need every piece to get you down the mountain safely. Those blocked paths and precipitous crevices force your expedition into uncharted territory. You'll need a guide who knows the landscape well enough to see which pieces are missing, find them, and put them in the right place.

Your financial picture requires the same kind of guidance. A piecemeal approach to retirement will take some extra time to explore every crevice to ensure each piece is recovered. You don't want to miss a small pension you forgot from a position you had in your twenties. The right professional can help you navigate when the map is a puzzle. He can help you with your lost pieces, and if you start working with him early enough, he can keep your map from being torn.

We weren't created to worry about our future. The Bible says, "Therefore I tell you, do not worry about your life, what you will eat or drink; or about your body, what you will wear. Is not life more than food, and the body more than clothes? Look at the birds of the air; they do not sow or reap or store away in barns, and yet your heavenly Father feeds them. Are you not much more valuable than they? Can any one of you by worrying add a single hour to your life?"[2] But with all these dangers, it's easy to get caught up in anxiety.

No one can avoid every stumbling block on the mountain; however, I believe there's a way to make the trip safely. With the proper guide and a little knowledge, you can escape most of the deadly trails and avalanches. So, let's take a look at how we can climb this mountain called life and make the descent with as little pain and injury as possible. We might even find ourselves saving thousands, even tens of thousands, of dollars in unnecessary taxes during the retirement decades.

PART TWO
FOUNDATION

CHAPTER TWO

OVERCOMING THE CHALLENGES OF THE DESCENT

*The prudent see danger and take refuge,
but the simple keep going and pay the penalty.*
—Proverbs 22:3 (NIV)

One advantage Vincent and Vivan had when they started down Mount Rainier was their years of preparation. By gradually practicing for the highest peaks in the United States, they were able to reach the summit safely and enjoy the view on the way down. Another aspect of their fun adventure was rooted in the fact that despite their successful descent of twenty or thirty mountainsides, they recognized the value of having two guides with hundreds of climbs under their belts. They understood that mountain hazards come in two forms: natural and manmade.

Vincent and Vivian knew they couldn't do anything to get out of crossing the rough terrain. Snow in the heights, altitude sickness, and crevices happen naturally. On the other hand, many falls can be avoided with proper safety gear, hydration, preparation, and by listening to the experts.

Our financial journey follows the same sort of path. Any number of traps await those reaching the summit of their life, and even more present themselves in the distribution decades. However, like mountain climbing, with an experienced sherpa to lead the way and show you the ropes, the manmade hazards can be minimized or even avoided.

Navigating The Hazards of Social Security

Because of the ever-changing landscape of the glacier-laden trail, guides have more than one direct path to the summit. Each season brings a slight change to the trail depending on where the crevices and remnants of avalanches lie. If any of the climbers had asked Anthony about the ideal trail to the top of Rainier, his answer might have sounded vague.

Likewise, when the average person considers retirement, thoughts go to Social Security, and most imagine a single easy path. However, just like the shifting glaciers on Mount Rainier differ from day to day, the eight hundred clickable links on the Social Security Administration's website each offer a rule or regulation that makes the correct path difficult to discern.

Currently, you can begin collecting Social Security at age sixty-two, and nearly twenty-eight percent will begin claiming their benefits without proper counsel. Many just assume they should apply for benefits the moment they're eligible. Others collect because a family member or fellow worker said it was best.

Your Social Security statement will show your monthly benefit at your FRA (Full Retirement Age), which is between age sixty-six and sixty-seven. Most retirees have no idea their monthly benefits increase eight percent between ages sixty-six or sixty-seven and seventy if they wait until they can receive the maximum monthly benefit. When people become aware of the variables, they start to ask, "What is the optimal age to apply for Social Security?" Unfortunately, the answer is no more standard than the path down a mountain. The age at which you should begin drawing your benefits depends on your personal circumstances.

The longer you wait, the more money you'll get each month; however, those whose lives are cut short lose out on some of that income. Some need the money to live on at sixty-two, while others can get by without it until they reach seventy, so they max out their monthly distribution. To make an informed decision, you also need to estimate how much other income you might have from recurring revenue or your part-time job. Any job-related money you bring in before you celebrate that full retirement age birthday will affect your benefit.

We frequently talk to people trying to navigate the hazards associated with Social Security. Fortunately, I've spent twenty-five years learning the ins and outs of retirement, and as the laws change, I find new information. It's relatively impossible for someone coming into the retirement game to understand all the twists without some help. Our firm offers a Free Income Claiming Analysis to optimize your Social Security lifetime benefits, which can lead to hundreds of thousands of dollars of additional lifetime income.

Only about seven percent of pre-retirees and retirees have the ideal retirement situation—a pension, sufficient savings, and Social Security—and forty percent rely solely on Social Security.[3] Often, when people come to me, I wish I had met them about a decade before their retirement so they could be as prepared for their final thirty years as Vincent and Vivian were for climbing Mount Rainier. There is nothing worse than hearing, "I wish I knew these strategies years ago."

And those who assumed a simple call to their local Social Security office would help them decide have discovered that SSA employees are not legally allowed to give advice. They can only give you the paperwork and give you generic instructions on filling it out.

While many believe Social Security is the easiest part of retirement, like Mount Rainier, it's best navigated with a guide who has a grasp on all the laws and takes time to fully understand your financial situation and your future plans. I believe claiming your benefits at the right time is an extremely important decision. And if you're married, the need for a wise choice grows. We've experienced people leaving hundreds of thousands of dollars on the table by claiming too early.

Clearly, Social Security has no one-size-fits-all answer, and traveling with an experienced guide can give you greater success. However, just like the crevices aren't the only hazard on the mountain, Social Security is merely the first of the potential perils we'll face.

Becoming Aware of the Tax Traps

Winter on Mount Rainier can be deadly. The decrease in daylight and increase in snowfall creates a recipe for peril. Groves of smaller trees can become completely covered. Even snowshoes can't save you from the tree wells. Even rangers have fallen between the hidden pines, dangling and trapped until their companions can help them get out. Tax laws have the potential to provide these same kinds of hazards for retirees every year.

"You will pay fewer taxes in retirement" might be the biggest myth of the golden years. Even those who recognize the fairy tale have a difficult time imagining they could be paying more taxes from their retirement assets than they did when they worked for a paycheck. But depending on how you set your accounts up before you retire, you could pay more taxes in the twenty to thirty years after you retire than you did during your thirty or forty years of employment.

A large part of the problem is the many who find themselves in a higher tax bracket after they retire. Especially if they've done well on the way up, the combination of 401(k)s, IRAs, pensions, and investment funds can lead to higher taxes. Inflation accounts for the rest of the snowfall. If you have an $85,000 lifestyle in the years before you retire, inflation will require you to double that amount in fifteen to eighteen years. This means you've been pushed into a higher tax bracket and now pay at a higher percentage without increasing your standard of living.

401(k)s, Traditional IRAs, 403(b)s, and pensions all play into the tax hazard as well. These retirement savings accounts seem like a blessing when they lower your tax burden during your employment decades. Plus, employers usually offer matching funds. It would be foolish to turn down the free money. The funds grow tax-deferred. It sounds like a win-win until you reach seventy-three, and the Required Minimum Distribution (RMD)—a percentage of your IRA you must take whether you want it or not—forces you to withdraw fully taxable funds. Remember, the IRS wants your tax money before you die.

Additionally, the Required Minimum Distribution percentage increases every year for the rest of your life. These funds come in as regular income—not capital gains. This means they put you in a higher tax bracket. Not only do you pay a higher tax on those funds, but now your pension and Social Security income fall into the higher bracket. The IRS brings in billions and billions in tax revenue every year that is directly related to RMDs.

Unfortunately, someone with a $500,000 account at age seventy is likely to have an account worth $200,000 at age ninety because of the RMDs. If you're counting on the interest from that account for your monthly income, you'll soon find the declining balance will result in less income. It seems to be designed to make you poorer.

Obviously maximizing retirement contributions with a matching employer plan can make sense. People in their twenties, thirties, and forties love these plans. However, when I interviewed people in their fifties, sixties, seventies, and eighties, I found they hated them. Few were aware of the way the funds would affect the rest of their income or the amount of tax on their accumulated wealth. The key to making the most of this valuable resource is having a targeted discussion with a knowledgeable advisor in your fifties and early sixties before you plan to retire.

Like the guides who help climbers take the most advantageous trail up Mount Rainier, an advisor experienced in retirement funds and the associated taxes can help you decide if it's time to begin using other methods to invest as you get closer to retirement.

Your guide might encourage you to use Roth IRAs for some of your retirement savings. Tax preparers often try to avoid Roths because these don't offer tax savings when funded. In an effort to save you as much on your tax bill as possible when you're climbing up the mountain, they will recommend the pre-tax savings route. However, on the way down, many retirees find that having their entire retirement savings in a 401(k) or other pre-tax accounts and very little in Roth funds resembles taking your axe and shovel on the climb but leaving the crampons behind because they're uncomfortable.

Though you'll pay taxes on your Roth payroll deduction on the way up the mountain, this type of retirement savings has no tax penalty on the way down. In fact, as the law stands today, even the growth can be withdrawn tax-free. To go even further, if you want to leave your children or grandchildren an inheritance, they won't have to pay tax on it either.

Putting part of your retirement savings in a Roth IRA gives you an extra bucket to draw from after you reach 59½. Designing a Custom Income Blueprint optimizes your buckets so you can withdraw the amount you need to spend monthly and pay the least amount of taxes. This allows you to keep your income within a targeted tax bracket each year.

And the tax traps don't end when you're gone. Your money can fall victim to the IRS code after your death. Tax laws change often; still pre-tax money you put in your 401(k)s can place huge tax burdens on "non-spouse" beneficiaries. And just like when you took it out, when your children make withdrawals, these funds have the potential to push every penny of their income into a higher tax bracket. If your children happen to be on Medicare, it affects those premiums as well.

Our fiduciary standard means we assist each client by offering tax strategies or solutions that reduce taxes, and we work with them in their investment and retirement income planning. Every dollar you save in taxes goes back into your pocket. We want to help you avoid the tax traps you could potentially face during the "distribution decades" or that your family might encounter after you're gone. The Bible says, "Render to Caesar the things that are Caesar's."[4] But I don't think we should give him a penny more. I prefer to put that money in your pocket and let God multiply it. Think of all the good you could do for your family or your favorite charity if you had the proper planning to stay in the lowest tax bracket possible.

Longevity Risks

When Vincent and Vivian began their mountain hikes, the risks were small. Those peaks in Vermont posed no threat of avalanches, crevices, or altitude sickness. But with every increase in elevation, their level of danger rose. The green paths became more rocky, and dirt trails turned icy. The higher they climb, the greater their risk.

Our retirement path poses similar hazards. With the decline in pensions, more individuals are responsible for making sure their retirement accounts have adequate amounts for the distribution decades of the mountain. And with every advancement we celebrate in healthcare, we must plan for those funds to last a bit longer.

In 1935, when the Social Security Act went into effect under President Roosevelt, only about 6.7 million people were sixty-five or older. If they made it that far, they could anticipate living another five to ten years. In 1980, more than 26 million fell in that older American category with an average life expectancy of close to seventy-five.[5] Today, there is a fifty percent chance one or both spouses can live into their nineties or longer.

Past generations supplemented their pensions and Social Security with Certificate of Deposit (CD) income. In 1960, a $100,000 CD netted them the equivalent of a year's average income at a six percent annual return—a hefty addition to their regular retirement income. Today, no one will consider purchasing a CD to help them alleviate the longevity risk. At .5 percent interest, even a $2,000,000 CD wouldn't come close to the average annual salary.

A 2019 World Economic Forum report suggests that many retirees have only enough retirement savings to take them to age seventy-four if they opt for an age sixty-five retirement. And with nearly 10,000 Americans reaching age sixty-five every day, this poses a huge problem. Almost 70 million Baby Boomers are racing into retirement, which causes an economic problem for every pension and healthcare system. One survey found that 80 percent of Americans fear running out of money before they reach the end of their life.[6]

The goal of retirement is to provide an income that will last as long as we do. This is difficult if you aren't aware of the risks. Fortunately, our Valmark team designed a unique planning process called The Retirement Income Survival Kit™ (R.I.S.K.).[7] This Custom Income Blueprint I mentioned earlier is designed to help people understand and address the potential problems in their current situation. Decades ago, many people planned to retire at age fifty-five, but the current economic atmosphere requires more and more people to keep earning until their late sixties or into their seventies. When this is a choice, my team applauds and encourages it; however, we see it happen out of necessity too often.

We want to help people avoid this dilemma if at all possible. We explore how the sequence of returns risk or the way the market and the timing of withdrawals work together can affect your long-term retirement savings. Does your investment strategy need to be adjusted to match your age and longevity expectations? How will inflation affect your lifestyle if you live to be ninety? And how will healthcare play into this longevity risk?

Healthcare Considerations Can Feel More Like Everest

While the climbing season at Mount Rainier sees few avalanches, Mount Everest loses a few of her most experienced natives every year. In 2014, thirteen sherpas lost their lives in the deadliest avalanche in the history of Everest mountaineering. These tremendously experienced men were nearly through the dangerous Khuma region at the 19,000-foot mark when the ice storm pummeled them.

That's what thinking about healthcare feels like for many older Americans. Yes, Medicare kicks in at age sixty-five for most individuals; however, few realize seniors pay a premium for that coverage. And fewer still understand how the government calculates that premium. While most companies base insurance costs on age or family size, Medicare premiums are determined by the amount of income you had two years prior. If you happen to inherit the family farm, sell a business, or receive a nice bonus, that money will be included when they fix your monthly Medicare costs two years later.

Additionally, the Social Security Administration includes those pre-tax RMDs when they set your premium. That bit of income means a permanent increase in what you pay monthly for your health insurance. And if you happen to be just one dollar over the threshold, your premium could increase by thousands of dollars more per year.

For example, let's say Louis and Lola took $3,000 out of their 401(k) to pay for half of their Mount Rainier climb. They know they'll have to pay twenty-two percent in taxes, but the $660 will be worth it. What they didn't realize is that their income was only $1,000 away from the next Medicare threshold, so their premiums will go up by $2,400 in eighteen months. It has cost them $3,060 to make a $3,000 extra withdrawal. If they had taken enough to buy a new truck or put a new roof on the house, it would have also put them in the forty-one percent tax bracket. While no one likes a car loan in retirement—especially when you have the money right there in your investments, you'll often pay less in interest over a few years than you will in taxes to take it all out at one time.

And none of this takes into consideration out-of-pocket health care costs after you retire. Like Louis and Lola's Mount Rainier trip, withdrawing funds to pay those bills can increase your tax burden and your Medicare premiums. Unfortunately, not many think about these costs when they're in their forties.

One solution few put into place is a Health Savings Account (HSA). Normally, your employer will put funds in for you; however, you can put funds in there every year as well. It's the only triple-tax-free account on the planet. The money is pre-tax going in, growth is tax-deferred, and when you take it out, it's tax-free. It's very advantageous to build up your HSA prior to retirement. Then, when you're over sixty-five and begin to have health issues that face many older citizens, you have tax-free funds to cover them.

Every bit of this little-known information can be overwhelming—especially when it crashes in as unexpectedly as an avalanche. But now that you are aware of the challenges you might face as you make your descent, you'll be better prepared to ask the right questions and choose the best guide.

CHAPTER THREE

BE ON THE LOOKOUT FOR FALSE GURUS

*Where there is no guidance
the people fall,
but in an abundance of counselors there is victory.*
— Proverbs 11:14

On the fourth morning, the expedition woke at 3:00 a.m. so they could reach the summit and return to Camp Schurman while it was still daylight. The cold wind and lack of available coffee made the morning miserable. But when the group arrived at the summit several hours later, their fatigue immediately vanished. The silence felt almost eerie, but it seemed wrong to interrupt nature's beauty. Carrying all the gear across the crevices through high winds had been worth it. The photos they took couldn't possibly do justice to the awe-inspiring scene.

When the party finally turned to head back down, another group of climbers told the guides it looked like they were about to walk off the edge of the earth. Anthony chuckled. They weren't the first to notice the steep descent. For some reason, climbers never complained about the abrupt upswing in altitude on the way up. But the rate of rise looked more ominous on the descent. Even the spikes on the crampons didn't ease the hikers' hesitations.

Louis' misstep simply proved to this group their fears weren't entirely unfounded. As the crew slowly pulled the inexperienced climber up the embankment, the early rise time started to catch up with them. Aching muscles and fatigue plagued them. Fortunately, Anthony and Finn's encouragement and experience helped them pull Louis to safety. The guides knew the team would need a few extra snack breaks as they returned to Camp Schurman to spend one last night on the mountain. With each pause, the tension Louis' near disaster caused seemed to fade.

Not All Advisors Are Created Equal

When people climb the Himalayas, they look for a sherpa. Sherpas of the 1800s were known for their integrity, endurance, and expertise in high-altitude environments. They lived on the lower slopes of Mount Chomolungma—what we know as Mount Everest—and were instrumental in making Sir Edmund Hillary's legendary 1953 summit possible.[8]

Because so few understand the perils of traveling the financial realm with an inexperienced guide, finding an investment sherpa sits low in the list of priorities. I feel sick when I see how many people rush to the advice of gurus with no license. It's like asking the boy who sells tickets for the climbing wall at the county fair to lead you up Mount Rainier. Some of these self-proclaimed financial experts have sophisticated websites and huge followings and find themselves invited to speak on some of the biggest stages. They know a great deal about budgeting and basic spending but feel compelled to offer more advanced advice. Yet, because these hikers aren't licensed, they have no liability for bad information.

For instance, if you search the name of the most famous financial advice person and add the term "credentials" following his name, this is the message you'll likely find: "He isn't a licensed investment advisor, nor does he possess any professional credential like the Certified Financial Planner (CFP) designation." Without the accountability and regulations associated with the licensing required in the financial services community, these so-called internet experts don't have to live with the consequences of their poor advice. If I or one of my colleagues said some of the things these unlicensed and non-registered advisors share, we would likely face charges and/or lose our credentials. These fake sherpas are really marketing gurus charging between $200 and $500 just to sit in their virtual seminar or receive a couple of coaching calls.[9]

The other kind of advisors many use are various investment websites. If you have time to do a lot of research and just enjoy the sport of investing, this might be for you. However, oftentimes, these sites more closely resemble trying to use the map on your phone to maneuver a mountain.

Think about all the dangers of scaling the highest mountains with a cellular GPS. What will you do when you lose signal? Will that phone app know where the avalanche zones are? What will you do when you run into a crevice that wasn't there the day the satellite took the picture of the mountain? The dangers of this type of climb far outweigh the benefits of being able to go it alone and enjoy scenery the group missed.

Lone Ranger investing has similar pitfalls. That website doesn't know the specifics of your situation. It doesn't understand your health or your future plans. The only information it cares about is your credit card information and how much you want to spend. Experience and a personal interest in you and your future go a long way on a mountain climb as well as retirement planning.

Imagine how badly our climbers' adventure would have ended with an inexperienced guide on Mount Rainier. Emmons Trail offers only one place to pitch a tent—on top of a glacier. What if their guide hadn't recognized the sounds of the melting ice river or known to probe throughout the night to make sure crevices weren't forming under them? Sure, they had to get up after only an hour of sleep to release their tents from the icy surface, move them in the forty-five mile-per-hour wind, and re-secure them in a spot where the ice river had more stability. But considering the other option was to wake up as they dropped to the bottom of a huge shear in the glacier, the hour of lost sleep and the extra they paid for a diligent guide was well worth it. Ensuring you have the same kind of sherpa advising you on the way up as well as the way down the mountain will make at least as much difference.

Friends Don't Make Good Advisors

Some people develop a sense of loyalty when they've been with an advisor for most of their lives. Trusting a friend or long-time financial manager simply because you have a history and want to support them would be like asking your buddy who leads people on hikes through the local park to be your guide up Mount Rainier. Though anyone would commend your loyalty, most would question your judgment.

Asking your friend for Social Security advice can be as dangerous as trusting him with your life on a climb. In fact, when it comes to Social Security, many CPAs and tax attorneys don't have the answers. In their defense, CPAs aren't usually hard-wired to work proactively. They deal with the numbers in front of them, and they do it well. And keeping up with the tax regulations is a full-time job. Adding the retirement aspect would be overwhelming. Everyone puts pressure on their CPA to save them as much as possible every January. Sadly, the upfront savings can sometimes negatively impact your taxes on your way back down the mountain.

Trying to Navigate the Mountain Alone

Fortunately, Vincent and Vivian and the sibling pairs followed every instruction Anthony and Finn shared. They roped up when necessary and didn't argue when the guides warned against removing the crampons—the large, spiked contraptions they attached to the bottoms of their hiking boots—even when the terrain looked a bit more tame.

Louis and Lola slowed the group several times when they paused to catch their breath or had problems with ropes. If they had simply followed instructions without trying to do things on their own, the descent would have been easier. As it was, Anthony and Finn worried the two would end up having some kind of real catastrophe.

When you hike the foothills of the Alleghenies, self-guided tours work well, although even in Hocking Hills, Ohio, hikers look to the map the park provides for reference. I guess one question we need to ask ourselves is, "Do I want a foothills or Mount Rainier size retirement account?"

The financial industry offers as many types of advisors as the hiking world boasts guides. Self-guided hikes and the entertaining rock-climbing wall may be wonderful options if you never want adventure. However, the higher you climb, the more experience you'll want in your guide. Even Anthony and Finn wouldn't try to take a team to the summit of Mount Everest.

Sadly, many rely on their CPAs to guide them through the rough terrain of Social Security. Unfortunately, while each one has a vast knowledge of the tax laws, many don't understand all the nuances of claiming Social Security. It's understandable. There are a variety of factors involved in determining your personal best time to start receiving benefits, and not all of them are tax-related.

The Fiduciary Difference

All these retirement perils mean you need to find the best guide for your situation. Fiduciary seems to be the latest buzzword in the financial world. But this title is more than just another piece of industry jargon. By design, the industry mandates that a person qualified as a financial fiduciary put the client's best interests ahead of their own. This threshold is higher than verifying a product is suitable for a client. It means the fiduciary faces ramifications for failing to disclose conflicts of interest that may exist behind the scenes. Plus, they have an obligation to do what is right for the client. Failure to act in this capacity will more than likely lead to complex disciplinary actions from supervisory organizations or industry regulators.

Given the enormous amount of elder abuse and the complications surrounding finances after age sixty-five, the government has put legislation in place to protect older citizens. The Securities and Exchange Commission (SEC), the Financial Industry Regulatory Authority (FINRA), the Department of Labor, and other regulators have been putting increasing reporting obligations on those who work in the financial industry.

In order for a financial services professional to become a Certified Financial Fiduciary, the planner has to have been practicing for at least five years with a college degree. Each certified candidate has also completed training, passed the exam, and adopted the code of conduct. Additionally, these individuals have undergone a full background check and are in good standing with their state and federal licensures.

The thing that really sets a fiduciary apart is their commitment to always do what's in your best interest. I recently told my son, "Integrity is priceless," and fiduciaries bring integrity to the table.

Whether you appreciate the Bible or not, few will argue about the value of advice the book provides regarding finances. In fact, you might be surprised to find out the sacred text contains more tips about money, wealth, spending, and saving than any other subject. In Proverbs 13:11, Solomon wrote, "Wealth obtained by fraud dwindles, but the one who gathers by labor increases it." Financial integrity is important in Scripture, and it's vital to building great relationships.

Integrity doesn't mean we're perfect; however, it does mean when we make mistakes, we own them and do our best to rectify them. More than a decade ago, Warren Buffet sent a memo to his leadership that read, *"We can afford to lose money—even a lot of money. But we can't afford to lose reputation—even a shred of reputation."*[10] That's the mindset of a fiduciary.

CHAPTER FOUR

THE SECRET TO PUTTING THE MAP BACK TOGETHER

For which of you, intending to build a tower, does not sit down first and count the cost, whether he has enough to finish it.
—Luke 14:28 (NKJV)

Sarah, a fitness coach who has been hiking mountain trails for years, hosts a blog where she shares her adventures. She also teaches mountaineering and wilderness navigation classes. Still, she admits that overconfidence got the best of her on one climb. Without referring to her map, she set a course for her descent. After a few hundred feet, she realized her choices had taken her down the wrong side of the summit. But she'd gone too far to turn back.

With little daylight left and no axe to navigate the unanticipated snowfields, she had to regroup. Fortunately, her vast experience allowed her to detour and make it back to the base safely. But she admits being lost in the wilderness alone is no fun.[11]

Sarah used her adventure to help her readers understand the importance of maps and knowing how to read them. Lost and alone on the mountain, she had to reorient herself to find the best way down. Having a map in ten or twelve pieces that she had to put together before she used it could have proven deadly. With darkness closing in, she didn't need that kind of chaos.

Unfortunately, many people start down the mountain of life with a piecemeal map. It looks more like a game of Tetris than a retirement plan. Some don't even know where to find all the parts. They neglect to heed the advice of Proverbs, "Know well the condition of your flocks and pay attention to your herds."[12] While less dangerous than descending Mount Rainier without navigation, when you don't have a comprehensive picture of your retirement, you could miss out on enjoying all your income.

The Shifting Landscape

Mount Rainier is covered with glaciers—rivers of slowly moving ice. This means the terrain has the potential to be in constant motion. Though the shifts are nearly imperceivable, what you see in the Spring can be completely different just a few weeks later. The retirement landscape has been gradually moving in a similar way over the last few decades.

Forty years ago, retirees had a simple plan—sign up for Social Security and collect the pension they had worked so hard to build. They conveyed their future in terms of monthly income rather than assets. Our grandparents didn't think about saving tons of money because they didn't have to. Additionally, there's a good chance your grandfather spent all his working years at the same company. He didn't need a topographical retirement map because the path was straightforward. Retirement presented no forks in the road, turns, or surprises.

The retirement landscape looks significantly different today. In March 2015, pension plans cost employers an additional $2.42 to $8.00 per hour per employee, depending on the industry.[13] It's no wonder companies moved to individual retirement plans. However, this shift added complexities for the post-fifty-nine generations. Employees lost their guaranteed pension and were forced to decide how much salary to invest. Some had pre- and post-tax options. Other companies switched plans as time progressed.

After doing this for decades, I've met with numerous people who don't have this information handy. As I ask questions and we begin the discussion, they'll remember they worked for Company A, but it merged with Company B. And after they quit, Company C bought it out. We often hear, "I'm pretty sure I had a pension with Company A, but I'm not sure what happened to it after the merger."

One other significant detour in the retirement terrain is job longevity. Today, the average person changes jobs twelve times, working at each place of employment for about four-and-a-half years.[14] Rather than one pension to pull from at retirement like their grandfathers, they have a menagerie of 401(k)s, IRAs, pensions, savings, and more. And depending on the employers, these accounts could potentially be scattered throughout any number of investment firms or agencies. Some funds have stipulations about when you can withdraw them, how and when you can roll them over, and at what point the employer's portion of the investment is vested.

Another shift in the financial landscape lies in the stock market. "The market will rebound soon" is a common phrase; however, I've seen a few eras where the market went sideways for a long time. The shifting market can also be a determining factor in when you begin to collect Social Security. There's no way to know if you'll be retiring in an up market or a down market. What happens if, three months after you retire, your investments drop by more than fifty percent like they did in the early 2000s? If you're relying on two percent of those investments as part of your income, that amount just got cut in half.

This doesn't mean you shouldn't have anything market-related in your portfolio; however, it does prove that the diversification model is a great risk strategy. In fact, even the Bible recommends it: "Invest in seven ventures, yes, in eight; you do not know what disaster may come upon the land."[15]

This vast array of options looks like the variety of challenges you'll face above seven thousand feet. Glaciers, rock walls, crevices, shifting ice, avalanches, and more await, and each requires different equipment and skills. Using a single approach to this landscape is akin to scaling Mount Rainier with only a pickaxe and a shredded map.

Prepared for Every Risk

A climber's pack differs depending on the height of the climb. If you only intend to mount a low-elevation summit, you obviously need less than if you're heading to the top of Washington's highest peak. But as you look toward retirement, don't you want to go as high as you can before you start the descent?

Anthony, Finn, and the climbing team left the summit with plenty of time to get tents set again for their final night on the mountain. The adrenaline rush from reaching the top kept the group going strong for a time, but the descent uses an entirely different set of skills—and muscles—than the trip up. Schurman Camp was less than twenty minutes away when the weight of Lola's supplies finally took its toll. The terrain had grown rocky in the few places where the snow had melted. When she stumbled, the only thing that saved her head from crashing into a huge boulder was the large, awkward pack she had opted to carry—the same pack that gravity used to pull her down when she started to fall. "I need everything in here," she had insisted when Anthony suggested she lighten her load a bit before they started.

Finn examined her ankle and bandaged the scrapes on her arms. Her thick coat hadn't survived the sharp stones as well as Lola. "I think the ankle is just a bad sprain, but walking on it will be tricky."

"How will she get off the mountain?" asked Louis.

"Oh, Louis, I can walk," Lola insisted.

"Do you remember what I told you at base camp?" Anthony replied. Louis gave him a questioning look. "Our goal is not to get you to the top of the mountain; the goal is to get you back to your car."[16]

"We're going to carry you down to Schurman, Mrs. Windaker," Finn continued. "Then we can get a helicopter to lift you both out."[17] [18]

Vivian took Lola's pack while Vincent and the others carried the injured woman on a makeshift gurney for the last leg to the camp.

Had Lola listened to the guides and packed only what they suggested in the pre-trip planning flyer and training, she would have been more sturdy on her feet. Anthony and Finn wanted each participant to have the best experience possible, which meant optimizing their packs and limiting what they carried.

When we're planning to descend the retirement mountain, we need to understand everything in our pack. Lola didn't even know for sure what was in hers. She randomly put things in there until it was full. So, though she had an impressive list, she actually made it more difficult to descend the mountain.

In the financial world, this would be the same as having money stuffed under every mattress in your house with a bit in several banks and investment firms and calling it your retirement plan. A fiduciary advisor can help you make sure everything in your portfolio is optimized. The most valuable thing you can have to navigate the shifting landscape of your income allocation years is a professional who can see your entire retirement picture. The right guide can take your pensions, 401(k)s, IRAs, savings, investments, bonds, and more and create the perfect map to get you down the mountain in the most efficient way possible.

This pack aspect is also why we need a great guide for the way up the mountain. If we have too little, we may not be able to access as much income on the way down. Too little preparation also means we run the risk of running out of funds before we finish our journey.

A Plan Is Essential

I often ask folks, "When will you stop needing money?" The answer is obvious; however, do you have a plan in place that will take you comfortably to that day when you don't need money anymore? And the planning can't ever stop. You wouldn't go five years without changing the filters in your furnace or changing the oil in your car. Yet, many people haven't talked to their financial advisor in at least that long. Retirement plans need constant attention, and we prefer Quarterly review chats to make certain we're still on track.

You have 8,760 hours to spend every year. When I talk to people about their future, I like to ask, "How many of those hours have you spent thinking about your financial life after retirement?" Most tell me they invested more time planning their annual vacation than they did getting ready for the final thirty years of their life.

Louis and Lola had put the bare minimum into preparing for their adventure, and their lack of planning showed. But even with a great plan in place, things don't always go as scheduled. Think about how much worse off the couple would have been without guides who knew what to do when they had to adjust.

Most mountain climbers are advised to set a "turn-around time" as part of their plan. This is the point at which you quit regardless of how far you've come. It keeps the climbers from ending up at a cold, windy summit at nightfall or using all their energy on the ascent, leaving nothing for the trip down.[19] Professional climbers plan for everything from the base camp to the summit and back again. They spend hours and hours going over the route, considering the current weather conditions and landscape, and mapping out the best route up and down the mountain. Even with all that planning, they know life happens. The "turn-around time" sets a boundary so they can safely make the round trip.

We need similar cushions and considerations in our retirement plans; however, if we don't know the full picture, we can't put all the factors into play. That's why having a clear map with "turn-around times" built in is essential as you begin to descend your mountain of life.

The risks you face as a retiree are as many as the challenges on the mountain. The Custom Income Blueprint planning process can bring more confidence and clarity to your future. After you put together the puzzle of your assets so you have a complete map, your Custom Blueprint matches them with different inflation rates based on your specific expenses. This allows you to determine how much of those assets you can take as income each year, so you have enough to last as long as you do (and your spouse if you're married).

Sadly, too many have not assessed the potential pitfalls of their retirement years. Many factors contribute to the percentage you can take and how long you can expect your assets to last. Your advisor should review a few standard items:

1. How easily can you access your assets? Do they have flexibility with regard to when and how much you

can withdraw? Will you have a Required Minimum Distribution?

2. How long do you expect to live? While many use their family's history to get an idea of their longevity potential, this number can be as unpredictable as the wind speed on the summit of the mountain. Despite the unknown, your plan needs to include a solution to the longevity risk.

3. What will your returns look like if there is a major economic crisis? A diversified portfolio may help minimize this risk, but the market offers no guarantees.

4. What will inflation look like over the next thirty years? Inflation is like a virus. It's inevitable and hits you differently every time it comes around. We can generally count on three or four percent inflation every year; however, we've seen years with double-digit inflation, and we need to be prepared.

5. Will you or your spouse need long-term care? Taking care of our health plays a significant role in what we can expect for our retirement years, and unforeseen falls, diseases, and more can affect how much money we will have to live comfortably as we age.

6. How will your surviving spouse be affected? If you have a pension, the risk of making poor choices might not be realized until after you're gone. Similarly, the way your other assets are set up when you're at the top of the mountain affects your spouse and perhaps your children. Early planning makes a difference.

Another planning process, Achieve Retirement Clarity (A.R.C.), assists our clients as they climb the mountain. By asking specific questions and consulting with a knowledgeable fiduciary professional, you can optimize your Social

Security benefits and create the perfect Hybrid retirement plan.

FinancialSecurity.org reports that happiness in retirement is based almost 100 percent on guaranteed lifetime income, not assets.[20] It's true: on the way up the mountain, we focus on assets, but on the way down, it's time to change our point of view and concentrate on how those assets produce enough to live on. By looking at every asset you've worked hard for since you started working, we can evaluate your potential future. Is it best to pull from your IRA or your 401(k) this year? How can we use your home equity most advantageously? Your rate of withdrawal can become a major risk as you descend the mountain.

At Secure Future Advisors, we work hard to put a Guaranteed Lifetime Income in place for our clients. We want our clients to have what Thomas Hegna defined as a Pay Check—money you use to cover your basic needs—as well as a Play Check—funds to cover retirement travel, new cars, and all the fun things you have planned for your golden years.[21] This can only be done when your advisor has the entire map in front of him. That's why we help you find all the pieces and put them together.

On the day you retire, all the rules change. Tax laws, risks, and the way you look at your assets morph into something new overnight. Two questions remain at the forefront as you start your descent:

1. How much guaranteed income do you need? (or have?)
2. Have you taken the key retirement risks off the table?

CHAPTER FIVE

IT'S TIME TO HAVE A CANDID CONVERSATION™

*But all things must be done properly
and in an orderly manner.*
—*1 Corinthians 14:40*

Secure Future Advisors™ enjoys working with folks to optimize their present as well as their future. As an independent fiduciary, our philosophy offers a comprehensive approach. I just don't see a way to do investment planning and retirement income planning without also providing tax planning. That's why we started our sister company, Secure Future Tax Advisors. This means we have knowledgeable tax consultants on hand, working together with our investment and retirement specialists to provide our clients with the highest level of service.

We believe every person was created to have the best life possible, and we have a passion for helping people navigate the mountain of life so they can achieve just that. We have two phases that include a total of five steps to help you reach your financial goals.

Every person is unique. Your future plans won't look exactly like anyone else's. Some want to travel; many look for ways to leave a legacy for their grandchildren or an organization they have a heart for. Others start a new hobby, dive deep into one they've been putting off for years, or even go back to school. The possibilities are endless as long as you're prepared.

Hopefully, you're reading this book at least ten years before you plan to retire. Don't worry; there's still hope for you if you're closer than a decade, but it's most beneficial for you to begin early.

You Need a Coach

Every professional athlete and Olympian has a coach. They know if they want to keep getting better, they need someone to push them—a person with more knowledge about their sport. Likewise, entrepreneurs and business people who want to keep scaling enlist the help of a mentor. I love the wisdom I receive from Strategic Coach® as well as the opportunity Dan Sullivan's team gives me to network with so many growth-minded individuals.

I love being a financial coach for those climbing and descending the wealth allocation mountain. While many feel as though all this planning and juggling is a burden, I call it fun. Like a teen playing a strategy game, I love the challenge of putting all the pieces in place to give my clients the best possible outcome. By using this God-given gift, I believe I'm serving my Creator the way Paul suggested, "Whatever you do, work at it with all your heart, as working for the Lord, not for human master."[22]

Every relationship I currently have started with a Candid Conversation™. It doesn't matter where you live—if you need a financial mountain guide, I'd love to hear your story. Our forty-five- to sixty-minute get-acquainted chat can happen over the phone, in person, or virtually. It simply gives us a chance to determine if we're the right fit for one another. I recommend this step regardless of the advisor you choose. You need someone who understands your picture of the future and aligns with your values.

We explore how we can help you have a "bigger future" by capturing opportunities as well as defining which future goals are most crucial for you. We break those milestones into those you want to meet over the next few years and ones you look forward to reaching in the decades to come.

At Secure Future Advisors, we work with professionals and small business owners, whether they are retirees or pre-retirees. Our "Right Fit Clients" don't like to lose money and aren't easily swayed by what I call "financial pornography"—fads and social media trends. They have a mindset that includes mutual trust and respect, a willingness to invest time with us, and a team approach to planning. Like athletic coaches and life coaches, we need people who are teachable and coachable. Otherwise, we simply can't help.

Some come to us looking for an investment planner, but we like to call ourselves income planners. Yes, we manage investments, but our goal in that endeavor is to give you a plan for optimal income with as much tax savings as possible as you descend the mountain. If you have funds invested through banks, you'll discover they do not offer tax advice. In all likelihood, they'll send you to a CPA who knows very little about the intricacies of how investments, retirement savings, and taxes intertwine.

One of my gifts is the ability to see how a client's financial accounts and lifestyle choices fit together, which includes Social Security, pensions, Medicare and long-term health care planning, investments, cash, rental income, business income, and any other sources of revenue during the descent down the mountain. An investment manager focuses on how to best make the portfolio grow, while an income planner focuses on growth that will give you the best life possible when you need to begin to make withdrawals.

The Candid Conversation allows our team, as well as potential clients, to make an informed decision about next steps. It offers insight into our values and expertise and gives both parties a feel for how we will work together. If we decide we should move forward together, we schedule The Evaluation Snapshot™.

Next Steps

Creating The Evaluation Snapshot may be one of my favorite parts of the process. This free strategy session in our unique planning engagement helps us understand your current financial picture. We identify places of greatest opportunity as well as strengths and potential obstacles. For instance, will your home be paid off before you retire? Do you expect to get a new car every few years, or do you lease a vehicle? We take into consideration your last couple tax returns and what kind of expenses you have outside the typical utility, food, health care, and insurance.

Other things we discuss include your family and charities. Do your grandchildren live close, or do you want funds to visit them a few times a year? What donations do you currently give? Do you plan to travel for missions?

Everyone comes to us wondering how much money they'll have to live on after they retire. Most have heard you can expect to pull out four to five percent of your retirement assets each year. Sad to say, that's a myth. Each person's situation is one-of-a-kind.

Sometimes, it's a challenging to inventory all the potential retirement income sources, but these pieces of the puzzle are essential to plan properly. This will include rental income, pensions, 401(k)s, IRAs, Roth IRAs, personal savings accounts, and any other assets you might have.

We encourage everyone to set up online access to their Social Security benefits and bring those statements with them when we meet. Additionally, we provide a customized Social Security assessment tool to help clients determine the most advantageous window to begin to take those benefits.

Often, we'll come out of this session with four or five suggestions on how to tweak or reconfigure the person's financial picture to take advantage of tax laws and avoid other retirement traps. Because we want to be completely transparent, those who decide to work with us receive our Clear Expectations Engagement Letter™ up front. This outlines our planning expectations and next steps, along with estimated fees.

We call the third step in Phase One The Clear Direction Navigator™. After we gather all the pieces of your retirement puzzle in our Income Claiming Analysis, we can put them together into a complete picture and provide you with The Roadmap of Recommendations™ and your Custom Income Blueprint. This is your unique plan based on your age, current financial status, when you plan to retire, and what you want to do post-retirement. We take into consideration your pre-retirement needs as well as the amounts you want in your Pay Checks and Play Checks. Your Play Check is a license to spend and enjoy decades of saving and investing.

Our Stewardship Principle says, "Proper education coupled with sound financial principles can bring more confidence and clarity to your future." We want this document to provide that clarity and confidence. We encourage questions and continued dialogue so you feel like you understand each component of your plan.

At the end of Phase One, you will have a completely organized system of your financial affairs and an action plan designed to solidify your current position.

Phase Two

When engaged for advisory services, Phase Two of our plan allows us to build a genuine, forever relationship. We don't want to just manage your money and make sure you have enough income. Our goal is to help our clients develop best financial practices and modify behaviors that can be detrimental to their future. As I said, we want to coach. My team wants to help people develop a full life—not just financially stable, but also emotionally stable.

Each quarter, we'll slow you down just a bit so you can review your plan. Then, we'll provide a list of action items our team will expertly manage. If you maintain other advisor relationships, we'll connect with these individuals on a regular basis to ensure all the pieces move together like a well-oiled machine. We know some of you have advisors who only want to meet once a year or every couple of years, but with the speed at which things change and move, you probably feel like you're starting over every time you meet. If you're busy—and who isn't—you may think quarterly is too much. But when you see how you can save and how much more you can do with your money, you'll see that it's worth it.

The reason we work so hard on an income and tax strategy is that we want the plan to do what it's supposed to do—help our clients build a more secure future. The portfolio, solutions, and products are mere servants to the plan. Many people get that backward. They are forever serving their investments. But that's just another example of the broken model that's been built around retirement.

Just like a mountain climbing adventure, this is not a one-and-done plan. Markets, laws, and life conditions change as readily as the wind and the weather. And much like your mountain guide will redirect your path to the safest, most advantageous route when necessary, we'll adjust our course only when needed. If your current advisor devises a map for you and doesn't intentionally review it on at least an annual basis (we recommend quarterly), it might be time for an honest evaluation of that relationship.

Our Stewardship Review™ provides ongoing conversations and guidance throughout the lifetime of your relationship with us. Not only do we simply review your portfolio and make suggestions, we believe in a culture of lifetime learning. To that end, we also encourage your participation in The Wisdom Builder Advocate™. We know that knowledge and wisdom are not the same thing. This ongoing education gives you information and provides ongoing advice to further your financial understanding and help you develop confidence.

Classes and Seminars

I enjoy educating people on the nuances of retirement and taxes, and I work with the American Financial Education Alliance (AFEA) to present free webinars and in-person classes at least monthly. One of the classes I lead is called "Savvy Tax Planning." Many times, people will come up to me afterward and say things like, "I wish I'd known that ten years ago . . ." "I didn't know I could . . ." "I've never heard of these tools." There's just so much involved in taxes and so many moving parts in planning for your future, it's impossible to know it all unless you're dedicated to it.

One gentleman stopped me after one of my classes and said, "You might be my missing piece." He had a great CPA to take care of his taxes, but no one was helping him create income strategies to take him to the end of his life. I like thinking of myself and my team as the missing piece.

Money as a Growth Tool

Life is a growth process. As long as we breathe, we can learn. The Bible tells us money can be a tremendous piece of that learning puzzle.

1. **God tells us our finances are a tool for growth.** Philippians 4:11-13 (NIV) says, *"I have learned to be content whatever the circumstances. ¹² I know what it is*

to be in need, and I know what it is to have plenty. I have learned the secret of being content in any and every situation, whether well fed or hungry, whether living in plenty or in want. [13] I can do all this through him who gives me strength." Contentment, regardless of the amount of money you have, is the highest level of living. Earlier, I mentioned the statistic that happiness in retirement is almost 100 percent dependent on income. At the same time, I've known many wealthy people who have no joy and others in poverty who live with great contentment. Jesus said we should put our money to work until He comes.[23] Money can improve life, but when it controls our happiness, it's not a tool; it's a weight. Money without contentment means we'll never be satisfied. Paul told Timothy, "But godliness actually is a means of great gain, when accompanied by contentment."[24] However, when we learn to be content and view godliness as our greatest goal, we can use our finances to improve the lives of the less fortunate and find joy in our growth.

2. **God tells us our finances are a test to help us grow.** Jesus said, "So if you have not been trustworthy in handling worldly wealth, who will trust you with true riches?"[25] If we've been blessed with wealth, we have a responsibility to use it wisely. Learning how to handle worldly wealth teaches us to be prepared for the riches of heaven.

3. **God can use our finances as a testimony.** Matthew 5:16 (NIV) tells us, "In the same way, let your light shine before others, that they may see your good deeds and glorify your Father in heaven." After we've learned how to handle wealth and be content in all circumstances, we can use our finances to show others how much Jesus loves them. One of the reasons I love to

give is because God has given so much to me. I want to use my finances to make the most of life, be the best person I can, and show people around the world the beauty of Christ.

Find Someone to Invest in You

You deserve to have someone who cares enough to invest time with you and walk with you as you navigate the challenges and changes that occur every year in the tax and Social Security realms. We want you to have a Secure Future personally, professionally, financially, and spiritually. Our strategies and solutions can turn uncertainty into certainty. Different than many others in our industry, our focus is on each individual's ideal plan. I can't guarantee my teams are the smartest on the planet, but I can tell you, you won't find a crew who cares more. We love building strong, genuine relationships that last generations.

At Secure Future Advisors and Secure Future Tax Advisors, we strive to turn your assets into a tax-efficient, sustainable income that keeps pace with inflation. It's not an easy task, but we know you need a plan to make your assets live for decades. Our goal is to become A Partner You Can Depend On™ for generations to come.

EPILOGUE

Camp Schurman sits at the 9,460-foot altitude mark, so everyone could breathe a bit easier again by the time they arrived. But the extra oxygen didn't make staking the tents any less stressful. They could clearly see the large crevice that had formed just after Anthony had them move their tents the night before. Between the twenty-five-mile-an-hour winds and the ice of the glacier, they felt like they had accomplished a feat when they got their sleeping quarters firmly pitched. After a high-carb dinner, they slept well despite the noises that came from the glacier bed.

The helicopter for Louis and Lola arrived just before the rest of the party began the final five-thousand-foot descent. Finally able to move at a reasonable pace, they arrived at the bottom about a half hour ahead of schedule.

Louis and Lola were the lucky ones. Though they had to be flown back to their car and had a hospital visit ahead of them, they made it back to the base alive.

Mount Rainier has fewer casualties than Mount Everest, and more bodies lay in the frozen ridges of the Himalayas than in Washington state, but in both cases, the descent is significantly more dangerous than the ascent.[26] And even more so when you're not quite prepared.

The last four miles, though almost even terrain, felt excruciating for everyone—probably because they knew they were getting close to the end. The entire group had a moment of celebration when they made it back to their cars.

Even after two hours in the car, their adventure still felt a little surreal to Vincent. "We did it, Vivian. Can you believe that view?"

"I wonder how the Windakers are. I'll check on them after we get home. I'm glad we exchanged phone numbers BEFORE we made the climb."

"We might have been as bad off as them if we hadn't had so much time on those summits over the last twenty years."

"Maybe. But did you notice how often they disregarded Anthony's warnings? From the moment he suggested Lola lighten her pack, they acted like they knew more than the guides. I really thought they must have climbed at least a few 14ers the way they talked."

"Anthony and Finn really knew what they were talking about. I'm glad we had experts leading the expedition."

With the right guides, the climbers made it back home to tell the stories of their adventure. It wasn't an easy trip, but they enjoyed every moment. They felt alive! Likewise, if you prepare and employ the right guides, you'll be able to spend your distribution decades with as much joy and fun as Vincent and Vivian's mountaintop trip. In fact, you might find yourself asking your spouse or friend the same question Vivian asked Vincent, "So, which mountain are we taking on next?"

ENDNOTES

1. *Pension Rights Center.* "How Many American Workers Participate in Workplace Retirement Plans?" March 2023, Accessed August 23, 2024. https://pensionrights.org/resource/how-many-american-workers-participate-in-workplace-retirement-plans/

2. Matthew 6:25-27 (NIV)

3. *National Institute for Retirement Security.* "New Report: 40% of Older Americans Rely Solely on Social Security for Retirement Income. January 14, 2020. https://www.nirsonline.org/2020/01/new-report-40-of-older-americans-rely-solely-on-social-security-for-retirement-income/.

4. Mark 12:17

5. *Social Security.* "Live Expectancy for Social Security." Accessed August 23, 2024. https://www.ssa.gov/history/lifeexpect.html.

6. *Protected Life Income.* "Are You at Risk of Outliving Your Money?" Accessed August 23, 2024. https://www.protectedincome.org/longevity-risk-expert-series/.

7. *Valmark Financial Group®.* "Wealth Management." Accessed August 23, 2024. https://valmarkfg.com/site/project/the-retirement-income-survival-kit-risk/

8. Sherpa, Serku and Wengel, Yana. "The Sherpas and Their Original Identity." 2023: Cambridge Scholars Publishing. https://www.cambridgescholars.com/resources/pdfs/978-1-5275-9439-5-sample.pdf.

9. *Ark Royal Wealth Management.* "What You Should Know About Dave Ramsey's Investing Essentials Virtual Event." March 12, 2024. https://ark-wealth.com/blog/what-you-should-know-about-dave-ramseys-investing-essentials-virtual-event.

10. Strong, Frank. *Sword and the Script.* "Warren Buffet Underscores the Value of Reputation." December 23, 2014. https://www.swordandthescript.com/2014/12/warren-buffet-reputation/.

11. Sarah. *Miss Adventure Pants.* "How to Navigate the Wilderness Like a Boss." April 30, 2018. https://missadventurepants.com/blog/wilderness-navigation-techniques.

12. Proverbs 27:23

13. *U.S. Bureau of Labor Statistics.* "Beyond the Numbers." February 2016. https://www.bls.gov/opub/btn/volume-5/trends-in-employer-costs-for-defined-benefit-plans.htm

14. Kolmar, Chris. *Zippia* "Average Number of Jobs in a Lifetime [2023]: How Many Jobs Does The Average Person Have." January 11, 2023. https://www.zippia.com/advice/average-number-jobs-in-lifetime/

15. Ecclesiastes 11:2 (NIV)

16. Chevassus, Beau. *Beau's Blog.* "Emmons Glacier Route from Camp Schurman, Mt. Rainier Summit Trail." July 29, 2019.

17. Sarah, *Miss Adventure Pants.* "This is what happens when you climb Mount Rainier without a guide." April 26, 2019. https://missadventurepants.com/blog/climb-mount-rainier-emmons-glacier.

18. *National Park Service.* "Mount Rainier National Park Completes Third Helicopter Rescue and Sixth Search and Rescue in Three Weeks." June 29, 2016. https://www.nps.gov/mora/learn/news/sar_6-29-2016.htm.

19. Onwuchekwa, John. *Four in the Morning.* "Most People Die on the Climb Down." January 24, 2023. https://www.johno.blog/p/most-people-die-on-the-climb-down.

20 Hegna, Tom. *Financial Security.org.* "Focus on Retirement Happiness to Make the Annuity Case." June 16, 2021. https://security.naifa.org/blog/focus-on-retirement-happiness-to-make-the-annuity-case.

21 Hegna, Thomas. *Pay Checks and Play Checks.* 2011. Acanthus Publishing.

22 Colossians 3:23 (NIV)

23 Luke 19:13

24 1 Timothy 6:6

25 Luke 16:11 (NIV)

26 Onwuchekwa, John. *Four in the Morning.* "Most People Die on the Climb Down." January 24, 2023. https://www.johno.blog/p/most-people-die-on-the-climb-down.

ACKNOWLEDGMENTS

I would like to thank my wife, Kelly, who has blessed me with 34 years of marriage. Kelly says I have the gift of aggravation, which is true since I am a middle child.

My nine wonderful children, ages 18 to 38, who have taught me more about life than anyone else.

Heartfelt thanks for all my entrepreneurial friends around the globe, who have encouraged me to focus on the fascinating and motivating future.

Finally, to our clients, who demand that we partner with them in planning for a more secure future. To all future readers, this book is designed to solidify your current situation.

ABOUT THE AUTHOR

Mark founded Secure Future Advisors and Secure Future Tax Advisors to help small business owners, successful professionals, pre-retirees, and retirees build a more secure future. He resides on a small family farm of ten acres in Waynesville, Ohio. He and his wife, Kelly, have been married for thirty-two years and have nine children, three of which are siblings adopted from Ethiopia. Together, the family raises miniature donkeys, chickens, horses, and bees. Mark participates in numerous non-profit ministries, including A Child's Hope International, a ministry focused on orphans and children around the world.

SECURE FUTURE ADVISORS™
Partners you can depend on

FREE STRATEGY SESSION

SECURE FUTURE ADVISORS IS A RETIREMENT PLANNING AND FINANCIAL SOLUTIONS COMPANY DEDICATED TO PROVIDING YOU WITH UNIQUE PROCESSES, TOOLS AND INVESTMENT AND INSURANCE SOLUTIONS.

ALTHOUGH OUR PROCESS IS INNOVATIVE, OUR TEAM BELIEVES IN A CONSERVATIVE APPROACH TO INVESTING YOUR MONEY AND ALLOCATING YOUR HARD EARNED RETIREMENT SAVINGS.

SecureFutureAdvisor.com

SECURE FUTURE ADVISORS™
Partners you can depend on

LET'S HAVE A CANDID CONVERSATION ABOUT YOUR VALUES & YOUR PRIORITIES TO SEE IF WE ARE A "RIGHT-FIT" FOR EACH OTHER.

SecureFutureAdvisor.com

THIS BOOK IS PROTECTED INTELLECTUAL PROPERTY

The author of this book values Intellectual Property and has utilized Instant IP, a groundbreaking technology. Instant IP is the patented, blockchain-based solution for Intellectual Property protection.

Blockchain is a distributed public digital record that can not be edited. Instant IP timestamps the author's ideas, creating a smart contract, thus an immutable digital asset that proves ownership and establishes a first to use / first to file event.

Protected by Instant IP ™

LEARN MORE AT INSTANTIP.TODAY

www.ingramcontent.com/pod-product-compliance
Lightning Source LLC
Chambersburg PA
CBHW052205070526
44585CB00017B/2078